## DATE DUE

| OCT 18, 2000 | |
|---|---|
| | |
| | |
| | |
| | |
| | |
| | |
| | |
| | |
| | |
| | |
| | |
| | |
| | |
| | |

# The
# Theodore
# Roosevelts

by
Cass R. Sandak

# CRESTWOOD HOUSE
New York

Maxwell Macmillan Canada
Toronto

Maxwell Macmillan International
New York   Oxford   Singapore   Sydney

**Library of Congress Cataloging-in-Publication Data**
Sandak, Cass R.
    The Theodore Roosevelts / by Cass R. Sandak. — 1st ed.
        p.   cm. — (First families)
    Includes bibliographical references (p.   ) and index.
    Summary: An account of the life of Theodore Roosevelt and his family, with emphasis on his years as president.
    ISBN 0-89686-634-3
    1. Roosevelt, Theodore, 1858–1919—Juvenile literature. 2. Roosevelt, Theodore, 1858–1919—Family—Juvenile
literature. 3. Roosevelt family—Juvenile literature. 4. Presidents—United States—Biography—Juvenile literature.
5. United States—Politics and government—1901–1909—Juvenile literature. [1. Roosevelt, Theodore, 1858–1919.
2. Presidents. 3. Roosevelt family.] I. Title. II. Series.
E757.S2    1991
973.91'1'092—dc20
[B]                                                                                                     91-7377
[92]                                                                                                         CIP
                                                                                                             AC


**Photo Credits**
Cover: Theodore Roosevelt Collection, Harvard College Library
Theodore Roosevelt Collection, Harvard College Library: 4, 7, 8, 9, 10, 13, 14, 16, 19, 20, 22, 24, 28, 34, 35, 37, 38, 39,
40, 41, 44
The picture on page 11 is reproduced with permission of the Houghton Library, Harvard University and is part of
the Theodore Roosevelt Collection, Harvard College Library.
Sagamore Hill National Historic Site/National Park Service: 17, 30
The New-York Historical Society, New York City: 43

Special thanks to Wallace Dailey of Houghton Library, Harvard University.

Copyright © 1991 Crestwood House, Macmillan Publishing Company

Macmillan Publishing Company          Maxwell Macmillan Canada, Inc.
866 Third Avenue                      1200 Eglinton Avenue East
New York, NY  10022                   Suite 200
                                      Don Mills, Ontario  M3C 3N1

**CRESTWOOD HOUSE**

Macmillan Publishing Company is part of the Maxwell Communication Group of Companies.

Produced by Flying Fish Studio

Printed in the United States of America

First edition

10  9  8  7  6  5  4  3  2  1

# Contents

*The funeral procession of Abraham Lincoln. Theodore and Elliott Roosevelt can be seen looking out of the second-floor window of the house on the left.*

# A Solemn Day

It was a sad day in April 1865. All New York City had turned out for a solemn event. It was the funeral procession for Abraham Lincoln. The 16th president of the United States had been shot shortly before in Washington, D.C. The assassin was John Wilkes Booth. He had struck the president down while he and his first lady were watching a play at Ford's Theater. Now Lincoln's body was being taken around to major cities. It was New York City's turn to pay its respects to the deceased president. The cortege was making its way through Union Square.

Three small children watched the funeral procession from an upstairs window. They were in the Cornelius Van Schaack Roosevelt mansion. This large house occupied one full block at the southwest corner of Union Square. The oldest of the three children was six and a half. His name was Theodore Roosevelt. One of the children was a girl, Edith Carow. She was almost four. She and her family were close friends of the Roosevelts. The third child was Theodore's brother, Elliott. He was five.

The three young friends watched from an upper-story window of the Roosevelts' house. The tiny girl's view was blocked by her friends Elliott and Theodore.

Little did anyone suspect that one day Theodore would be president of the United States. Nor was there any reason to think that Edith Carow would one day be Theodore's wife and his first lady. And certainly it didn't occur to anyone that years later Elliott's daughter, Anna Eleanor, would be the wife of another president, Franklin Delano Roosevelt, and be his first lady.

It was a fateful gathering.

# The Young Theodore

Theodore Roosevelt is the only president who was born in New York City. The date was October 27, 1858. Theodore was his parents' second-born child. His sister Anna (Bamie) had been born in 1855.

Theodore's grandmother often sang a Dutch cradle song as she rocked her infant grandson. The lullaby had been in the Roosevelt family since the days of New York's early Dutch settlers. Theodore's mother, Martha (Mittie) Bulloch, had been born in 1835. She was raised on a plantation in the South.

The Roosevelt family had been settled in the Dutch colony of New Amsterdam (later New York) since the 1640s. Klaes Martenszen van Rosenvelt was Theodore's first ancestor in the New World. His descendants had gone through seven generations before Theodore was born. They rose to prominence in the commercial and social life of the city. Theodore's grandfather and father derived their wealth mostly from real estate and from importing glass from Europe.

*Theodore Roosevelt, age 11*

*The Roosevelt family while on holiday in Egypt in 1872. Theodore is in the front, second from the right.*

Roosevelt's father, Theodore Sr., was a large, kindly man. He had enough money to be able to retire early and devote time to his family and humanitarian projects. He served on the boards of several New York City hospitals and charities.

Theodore was a sickly child. Because of his asthma, he was tutored at home. He was able to master many subjects because he read widely. Early in his life, Roosevelt dreamed of devoting himself to literature. A busy career in public service intervened, but still Roosevelt found time to pen an incredible amount of material. Roosevelt's published writings extend from 1877 until the end of his life.

There was always a sense of liveliness around the Roosevelt home. Young Theodore once kept a dead mouse in the icebox. And his brother, Elliott, resented having to share his bedroom with snakes and other creatures both dead and alive.

Roosevelt's father had a tremendous influence on Teddy's development as a human being and "apostle of the strenuous life," as he has often been described. When he was about 12, Theodore heard these words of encouragement from his father: "You have the mind, but you haven't got the body. To do all you can with your mind, you must make your body match it." Theodore took his father's words to heart. He began a vigorous program of exercise and self-development.

It was at about this time that Theodore's father built an open-air gymnasium onto the back of their house on New York's 20th Street. All the young Roosevelts had health problems to overcome. Bamie had a spinal deformity. Theodore and Corinne (Conie) suffered from asthma. And brother Elliott had constant headaches.

*Theodore, Corinne and Elliott Roosevelt with their cousins Maude and John Elliott*

In 1869 the Roosevelts left on a yearlong journey that was to take them through Europe. They first visited Bulloch relatives in England. In October 1872 they left on another yearlong journey. This time they went to Egypt and the Holy Land before traveling to Vienna. There the senior Roosevelt was to be the American representative at the Vienna Exposition of 1873. When they returned to New York in November 1873, it was to a new, larger house uptown.

Roosevelt was 19 when his father died. Theodore said of his father that he was "the best man I ever knew." And this was long after he had spent a lifetime meeting with some of the most distinguished people in Europe and America.

In his devotion to duty, to high principles, to morality and to religion, Theodore Roosevelt fit the 19th-century idea of a gentleman. In his philosophy, life and beliefs, Roosevelt continued a tradition. He was born into a family of wealth and privilege. He possessed every social advantage. At the same time he was, strangely enough, a self-made man.

*Theodore Roosevelt's senior class picture*

*Theodore with Alice Hathaway Lee the year before their marriage.*

# Roosevelt's First Marriage

Theodore Roosevelt was educated at Harvard University. In 1880, the same year he graduated from Harvard, Theodore married Alice Hathaway Lee. The date was October 27, also his birthday. He had intended to become a naturalist. But after the wedding to Alice he decided to become a lawyer instead. He enrolled at Columbia Law School, but he did not graduate.

Roosevelt thought that the law would be a good way to enter politics. Family members and friends were shocked by his choice of a political career. But Roosevelt told them that he intended to be "one of the governing class." By the age of 23, Roosevelt found himself elected to the New York State legislature in Albany.

11

Theodore's wife, Alice, seemed to conform to an ideal of 19th-century feminine beauty. She was blond, tall, graceful and athletic, and she carried herself as a queen might. But the marriage was to be a short one.

At three o'clock in the morning on February 14, 1884, Roosevelt's beloved mother, Mittie, died of typhoid. At two in the afternoon of the same day, Alice Roosevelt died of Bright's disease, a type of kidney failure. A double funeral service was held at Fifth Avenue Presbyterian Church.

Roosevelt was 25 when his mother and his wife died. Two days before Alice died she had given birth to their only child, Alice Lee Roosevelt. Their marriage had lasted only three years and three months. His wife was 22.

Following the deaths of his mother and wife, Roosevelt returned to political life in Albany. There he was able to complete the legislative session. As soon as possible, however, he left for his ranch in Dakota Territory. He had purchased this property and some cattle the previous autumn.

For the next three years Roosevelt lived the life of a rancher. He spent long days in the saddle. He also served as deputy sheriff and led battles against cattle thieves. Roosevelt earned the respect of the cowboys he lived among. He could work side by side with the best of them. But in language and habits, he still remained an Easterner.

Roosevelt also found time while living on the prairie to write biographies of the statesman Thomas Hart Benton and of Gouverneur Morris, an early American political leader. He wrote two other books in this same period about the joys of ranching and hunting.

*Theodore riding on his ranch in Dakota Territory after the deaths of both his wife and his mother*

Roosevelt was called away from this idyllic life in 1886. The Republican party in New York City wanted Theodore to run for mayor. Roosevelt's bid for the office was unsuccessful, but his interest in public affairs was drawing him once more into political life.

*Edith Carow, age seven*

# The Young Edith

Edith Kermit Carow was born in 1861. Edith's family was American of English and French origins. Edith's mother, Gertrude Tyler, had been well educated at the best schools in Paris and New York. Mrs. Carow had been born in Somerset, a county in the west of England. She was related to several distinguished American and English families, including that of William Pitt. Pitt, one of England's most famous prime ministers in the late 18th and early 19th centuries, was a cousin.

The Carow family home in New York City was just off 14th Street, near Theodore's grandfather's house. Edith was best friends with Theodore's younger sister, Conie.

Edith took her lessons with the Roosevelt children at their home on 20th Street. Mrs. Roosevelt's sister Anna Bulloch was "Aunt Annie" to the children. She served as their governess. Even after she became Mrs. Gracie, Anna taught the Roosevelt children and their friend Edith in a classroom in the nursery of the Roosevelt home. Edith did not, however, join the Roosevelt children in their workouts in the open-air gymnasium.

After age 10 Edith was enrolled at Miss Comstock's School, a private academy for young ladies in New York City. Her main subjects were Latin, French, literature and English history. Training in religion and music rounded out the curriculum. The pupils did not receive much instruction in mathematics or the sciences. Edith developed a lifelong love of Shakespeare and of classical music. She stayed at Miss Comstock's until graduation, when she was 18.

In 1876, when she was 14, young Edith visited the White House. Mrs. Ulysses Grant had just completed the centennial redecorating of the executive mansion. Afterward, Edith wrote to Teddy's sister of the experience. "Today . . . I went to the White House. . . . How unlikely it is that . . . I shall ever come in contact with [it again]."

Edith took great pains to keep much of her childhood a secret. Her father was an alcoholic who steadily lost money. This brought the family's standard of living into a downward spiral. His family shipping business was in steady decline. Mrs. Carow tended to be depressed. For a period of time they lived with various families of relatives until they had outstayed their welcome.

*Edith, age 24, the year before her marriage to Theodore*

Edith and Theodore had been great childhood friends. And they had remained close throughout their teens. Then they drifted apart, as people do. And for a period of time they avoided each other entirely.

Edith was bitterly disappointed when she heard of Theodore's proposed marriage to Alice Lee. Still, Edith went to Brookline, Massachusetts, to attend the wedding. She managed to join in the dancing and to be a picture of grace and charm. But she kept her sadness to herself. She knew in her heart that she would someday be Theodore's wife.

# Roosevelt's Second Marriage

Theodore was 28 when he married Edith Kermit Carow. Theodore had once described her as "the most cultivated, best-read girl" he knew.

In 1886 Edith was living in England with her mother. Theodore went to England to see his childhood friend. After a brief courtship they were married in London on December 2, 1886. Shortly afterward they returned to the United States. By this time Sagamore Hill, the house that Roosevelt had planned for his wife Alice, was finished. Because she died before the house was built, Alice had never lived there.

The lavish home overlooking Long Island Sound at Oyster Bay had 26 rooms. It was ready to be moved into in 1887 when Theodore and Edith returned from Europe. There Edith managed a household staff of maids, a cook, gardeners and stable hands. Like the Washingtons' home at Mount Vernon, Sagamore Hill became the Roosevelts' favored retreat from public life.

*Sagamore Hill, circa 1885*

A frequent visitor at Sagamore Hill was Theodore's niece, Anna Eleanor Roosevelt. She was the daughter of Theodore's brother, Elliott. Theodore was as fond of her as if she were his own daughter. However, Theodore's own daughter, Alice, was just eight months older than Eleanor. And Alice was somewhat jealous of her father's closeness with her cousin.

Eleanor's relationship with her own parents was at best difficult. Her mother, who had always been overly critical of the girl, died when Eleanor was eight. Eleanor adored her father, Elliott Roosevelt, but he was an alcoholic. When Elliott died in 1893, Eleanor's visits to Sagamore Hill became more frequent. It was largely Edith Roosevelt's idea that the young girl be sent to a boarding school in England. This kept Edith from being excessively bothered by having to raise the girl, whose future prospects she doubted.

In fact, Eleanor became the wife of a distant cousin of Theodore's, Franklin Delano Roosevelt. When Eleanor walked down the aisle to become Franklin's wife in 1905, it was on the arm of her uncle, President Theodore Roosevelt. Eleanor Roosevelt went on to become one of America's best-loved first ladies.

In addition to Alice, the child of Roosevelt's first marriage, Edith and Theodore had five children of their own. They were Theodore Jr. (born in 1887), Kermit (born in 1889), Ethel Carow (born in 1891), Archibald Bulloch (born in 1894) and Quentin (born in 1897). When the Roosevelts moved into the White House in 1901, Quentin was four. The eldest, Theodore Jr., had just turned 14 the day before his father took office.

*Alice* (seated) *with Theodore Jr., Ethel, Quentin, Kermit and Archibald Roosevelt*

Edith Roosevelt was a quiet and elegant woman. She was the perfect contrast to her enthusiastic, larger-than-life husband. She referred to Theodore as her "oldest and rather worst child" or her "fifth boy."

Edith was a shrewdly intelligent and capable woman. Where Roosevelt was an idealist, Edith was practical and realistic. She had a tremendous influence over her husband. She controlled family finances and gave him a $20-a-day allowance for expenses! People were afraid to cross Edith— even the president was in awe of her. Edith avoided people she didn't like. While standing in receiving lines she usually held a large bouquet. This meant she wouldn't have to shake people's hands. As Alice said of her stepmother, she "usually called the shots."

*The headstrong Alice at age 18*

# Daughter Alice

Edith regarded her stepdaughter Alice as her most demanding personal challenge. The headstrong girl was more than a handful. As a frequent visitor to her maternal grandparents' estate, Alice enjoyed a certain independence. She spent three weeks of every spring and fall with her grandparents in Boston. Alice also showed a healthy adolescent defiance toward her stepmother.

At first Alice did not want to go to live at the White House. But her stepmother lured her there by promising her a spectacular debutante ball. Planning the debut for the end of 1902 brought Edith close to a nervous breakdown.

But Edith's troubles were only beginning. Alice quickly outshone her stepmother in the public eye. The press began calling her Princess Alice after she christened a yacht belonging to a German prince. She was the most talked-about woman in America and had a tremendous influence on her generation. Songs were written about her, and mothers named their babies after her. Even a color was named for her. "Alice blue" is a particular shade of blue-gray.

Alice was the perfect "Gibson" girl type: tall, healthy, athletic and active. Alice refused to go to boarding school. She smoked and she drove fast cars. In her rebellious attitude, she was almost ahead of her time. Her father said of Alice, "I can do one of two things: I can be the president of the United States or I can control Alice. I cannot possibly do both."

Alice's wedding in 1906 to Nicholas Longworth was the fourth White House wedding of a president's daughter. Sick of the media circus, Edith barred the press from Alice's wedding. She insisted that only invited guests be admitted to the ceremony and reception. (Franklin Roosevelt was among them.) Not a single photographer or reporter was present. But outside the press had a field day when Alice left the reception for her honeymoon.

Edith breathed a huge sigh of relief when Alice finally left on her wedding trip. Edith's parting words to her stepdaughter were: "I want you to know that I'm glad to see you leave. You have never been anything but trouble."

Alice remained a force in Washington social and political life well into the 1970s. As the wife and then widow of Congressman (and later Speaker of the House) Nicholas Longworth, she was a frequent guest at White House functions. Her dry sense of humor and her outspokenness—not to mention her pedigree—made her a popular figure in the nation's capital.

# The Road to the White House

Roosevelt's career in politics developed quickly. He was appointed to head the Civil Service Commission in Washington in 1889. As president of the Board of Police Commissioners, he returned to New York City in 1895. By 1897 he was back in Washington as assistant secretary of the navy.

By February 1898, Roosevelt was still serving with the navy. Suddenly the American battleship *Maine* was blown up in Havana harbor in Cuba. Within two months the United States went to war against Spain. At the outbreak of the Spanish-American War, Roosevelt resigned his position to help organize a volunteer cavalry regiment.

This cavalry unit was called the Rough Riders. As commander of the unit, Roosevelt led the successful charge of the Rough Riders in the Battle of San Juan Hill in Cuba.

*Theodore Roosevelt and his Rough Riders*

Roosevelt returned from the conflict a hero. As a result of the Spanish-American war victories, the United States acquired the Philippines, Guam and Puerto Rico from Spain.

By the end of September 1898, New York State's Republican party had named Roosevelt its candidate for governor. He won by a narrow margin and served as governor for two years. His administration was marked by mild reform legislation and strict adherence to ethical principles.

Roosevelt served as New York's governor until he was chosen as President McKinley's vice-presidential running mate. (His former vice president had died.) Roosevelt was reluctant to accept the offer because he thought that being vice president would take him out of active politics. He feared his chances would be weakened for the presidential nomination in 1904. But in the end he accepted the convention's nomination as McKinley's running mate.

# Becoming President

By 1901 the Roosevelts were installed in Washington as the second vice-presidential family under McKinley. The Roosevelts were a lively addition to the capitol's social life. It would be difficult to find a more eccentric couple than Ida and William McKinley. President McKinley was a tired and unhappy man who found the presidency a heavy burden. Mrs. McKinley was a semi-invalid, prematurely aged by sorrow over the deaths of their two young daughters. She also suffered from depression, migraines and fainting spells as well as epileptic fits.

When Roosevelt became president, it was not through an election. On September 6, 1901, President McKinley was shot in Buffalo, New York, while he was standing in a reception line. The shot was fired by Leon Czolgosz, a disgruntled anarchist. (An anarchist is a person who rebels against all authority.) Roosevelt received word of the attempt on McKinley's life while he was attending an outing of the Vermont Fish and Game League. He left for Buffalo immediately.

Roosevelt went to McKinley's bedside. Two days later, McKinley seemed to be improving. On September 10 Roosevelt left to join his family hiking in the Adirondack Mountains. The family was climbing Mount Marcy when word came on September 13 that McKinley was dying.

McKinley died, and on September 14 Theodore Roosevelt was sworn in by a U.S. District Court judge. At 42 he was the youngest president ever. Roosevelt's first action as president was to declare September 19 a day of mourning for President McKinley.

*Roosevelt entering the home of President McKinley shortly before the president's death*

# T. R. as President

With McKinley's assassination in 1901, the Roosevelts were suddenly catapulted into the limelight. Even though Edith detested the idea of life in the public eye, it was her handling of the role of first lady that helped shape the 20th-century notion of what a first lady should be.

The contrast with the McKinley administration was startling. And Edith Roosevelt was a good match for her husband. She too was young—only 40. Like her husband, she was an early riser. The two took brisk morning walks together, even in the coldest weather.

Edith Roosevelt was a retiring person who preferred solitude and quiet pastimes, such as reading, to socializing. She never coveted the role of first lady. In fact, she had attempted to dissuade Theodore from running for mayor of New York City and later from accepting the nomination to run for vice president.

The Roosevelt administration seemed to bring the 20th century to Washington political life. Although Roosevelt came to the presidency almost by accident, he was just what the country needed. He was young, optimistic and filled with energy and enthusiasm. The United States had changed enormously in the less than four decades since Lincoln's death. Industry and undreamed-of inventions were transforming the country. These included the telephone, the automobile, electric power, motion pictures and the airplane. The country was on its way from a sleepy agricultural nation to becoming an industrial power. Factories, steel mills and railroads were part of the phenomenal growth. But with that growth came new social problems. And Roosevelt set about to tackle them.

The Roosevelts came to Washington like a breath of fresh air after the McKinleys. They had been elderly and brittle. And during the McKinleys' time the White House had had a stuffy Victorian sickroom atmosphere.

Roosevelt's love of sports and strenuous recreations of all kinds continued all through his presidency. He invited professional boxers and wrestlers to work out with him during his years in public office. John L. Sullivan, the retired boxing champion, often sparred with him. The president was blinded in his left eye after a boxing partner's punch broke some blood vessels in it.

Roosevelt was the first president to talk regularly with reporters. And Edith Roosevelt was the first president's wife to have her own social secretary. Isabella (Belle) Hagner's salary was $1,400, paid for by the federal government.

Presidents' wives had traditionally been called "first lady of the land." Edith Carow Roosevelt was the first to be known simply as the "first lady."

As president, Theodore Roosevelt saw the United States grow to the status of a major world power. Because he had served as assistant secretary of the navy, he understood the navy's importance. As a result, he expanded America's power at sea.

He was also aware of U.S. interests south of the border. In November 1901 Roosevelt signed a treaty with Great Britain. The agreement gave the United States the right to build a canal through Panama, which would shorten the journey between the Atlantic and the Pacific oceans.

Fascinated with new technology, Roosevelt sent a wireless message to King Edward VII of England in 1903. The message was sent via the newly constructed Marconi station in Wellfleet, Massachusetts. Later, in 1905, Roosevelt became the first president to submerge in a submarine. His visit took him on board the USS *Plunger*. At that time the sub was on maneuvers not far from the presidential yacht *Mayflower*.

In his concern for the environment, Roosevelt was surprisingly modern. He was an early conservationist and railed against the custom of cutting down trees for Christmas. In fact, he once forbade Christmas trees in the White House. He relented when he learned that his son Kermit had secretly placed a tree in his bedroom, decorating it with ornaments and gifts. After that, the wishes of his wife and children prevailed and trees were allowed to be set up.

Roosevelt left an impressive legacy as a conservationist. He established the first federal bird and game refuges, and increased forest reserves by over 400%. He created five new national parks, started the first federal irrigation projects and set aside 18 sites as national monuments, including Muir Woods, Mount Olympus and the Grand Canyon.

Roosevelt was an enthusiastic hunter, but he was also softhearted and believed in fair play. On a hunting trip in 1902, Roosevelt and his party had pursued a bear for many miles. Some of the hunters then captured a bear and held it at the camp until Roosevelt returned. When they asked the president to shoot the bear, he refused and set the animal free. He didn't think it was fair to shoot a bear that had been tied up.

After the story was reported in newspapers, a toy manufacturer wrote to the president asking permission to call his company's stuffed bears "teddy bears." Roosevelt agreed. And a legend was born.

As president, Roosevelt continued to work for civil service reform. He sought to end strikes and to improve conditions for workers in various industries all over the country. And he fought against trusts and other abuses by big business.

*President Roosevelt confronts a teddy bear during commencement exercises at Cambridge University.*

# Life at the
# White House

When the Roosevelts came to Washington, the White House was shabby and run-down. The floors needed extra support every time there was a big reception. Edith found the house gloomy and the living quarters on the second floor far too cramped for her large, boisterous family. At that time the private living quarters consisted of only eight rooms.

It was suggested that a new executive mansion be built, but Roosevelt would not hear of it. He considered the White House one of the historic centers of the nation. He stated: "The president should live nowhere else but in the White House."

Living in the White House was not exactly to Edith Roosevelt's taste. Theodore reported to a friend: "Edie says it's like living over the store." Like Martha Washington, Edith Roosevelt was a public figure who wasn't really comfortable in the limelight. There was something secretive and reclusive about her nature. A former classmate once wrote of Edith: "I believe you could live in the same house with Edith for 50 years and never really know her."

Before Edith took on the task of refurbishing the White House, the East Room was a stuffy Victorian parlor, resembling nothing so much as a hotel lobby. It had the expected floral carpeting, tufted plush chairs and immense potted plants.

Mrs. Roosevelt engaged Charles McKim to transform the White House. McKim was a leading American architect of the time. He designed a new East Wing as an entrance for visitors. The West Wing was added to house the president's office and most other administrative offices. McKim also tore down the rambling greenhouses that had sprung up all around the White House.

Much Victorian clutter had been added in the 19th century. It was all stripped away and the mansion was left closer to its original gracious form. The State Dining Room was enlarged to accommodate increasing numbers of dinner guests. With McKim's help, the Roosevelts restored the White House to its former dignity and grandeur.

*The East Room of the White House after its restoration under the Roosevelts*

The White House restoration was completed in time for the New Year's reception on January 8, 1903. During the period of restoration the Roosevelts lived at nearby Townshend House. In justifying the restoration efforts in his 1903 report to Congress, Roosevelt called the White House "the property of the nation. It is a good thing to preserve such buildings as historic monuments which keep alive our sense of continuity with our nation's past."

Theodore Roosevelt changed the name of the Executive Mansion in 1901. Although for years it had been referred to by most people as the White House, in that year the title became official.

Edith performed her duties as White House hostess to perfection and did much to restore the mansion to its true 18th-century elegance. Edith also ordered construction of the tennis court to provide exercise for Theodore and the family.

The Roosevelts often invited dinner guests to the White House. Theodore Roosevelt paid the cost of White House banquets from his own pocket so that no one could criticize him or his wife for extravagance at the public expense. They served the finest dishes and costly wines and champagnes and provided musical entertainment. Roosevelt spent more on White House entertaining than any other president before him.

# The White House Gang

The Roosevelt years were a lively time in Washington. At the White House, visits from relatives, friends and other guests were frequent.

All the Roosevelt children lived in the White House—Theodore Jr., Kermit, Archibald, Ethel and Quentin. They were joined by their older half sister, Alice. The five younger members of the Roosevelt brood brought their own special brand of chaos to the White House. Because they were likable and young, they quickly became the darlings of the press.

Together with cousins and friends, the children rode their bicycles through the halls and slid down the carpeted stairs on trays. They also welcomed the chance to explore the attics and cellars of the historic home. The children would roller-skate over the polished wooden floors of the recently restored East Room. And Quentin walked through the house and gardens on stilts.

The children's menagerie included cats, dogs, mice, rats, raccoons, badgers, guinea pigs, parrots, snakes—and a bear! They even carried the calico Shetland pony Algonquin up and down the White House elevator. Quentin did this while Archie was sick in bed with measles. The sight of the pony certainly cheered up the sick boy.

Theodore Sr. often joined in the children's play. He would roughhouse with them, wrestling on the floor. Sometimes he set up a "point-to-point march" in which all obstacles had to be climbed or crawled over or swum through. Sometimes the whole family went out West for rigorous vacations. The Roosevelts were a big, active and close-knit family with many hobbies and interests.

Theodore wrote to one of his children: "I don't think any family has ever enjoyed the White House more than we have."

# Christmas with the Roosevelts

When they did not stay at the White House for Christmas, the Roosevelts always went to Sagamore Hill. They traveled by horse-drawn sleigh or car to the Episcopal Church in Oyster Bay for the Christmas Eve service.

The Roosevelts loved family life and children. They always bought vast quantities of Christmas presents. Usually each family member had his or her own table of presents set up in the drawing room. Stockings were also filled with small gifts. Often the Roosevelts composed special poems to accompany their gifts. Theodore Roosevelt loved to tell Christmas stories or read from Dickens.

At Christmas in 1902, Archie, one of the younger children, made sure that each of the family pets received a gift. In a letter, Theodore Roosevelt proudly wrote of his children's joy in gift giving. There was something for "Jack the dog, Tom Quartz the kitten, and Algonquin the pony, whom Archie would no more think of neglecting than I would neglect his brothers and sisters."

The Roosevelts followed a combination of English and Dutch customs. By the beginning of the 20th century these customs had blended into an American Christmas.

The Roosevelt Christmas dinner was at lunchtime. A roasted pig with an apple in its mouth was one of the most interesting features. The meal concluded with a flaming plum pudding, the traditional English Christmas dessert.

One Christmas Eve, Edith Roosevelt held a party at the White House for 600 children of officials in her husband's administration.

*Ethel and Archibald Roosevelt play in the snow at Sagamore Hill.*

*Theodore Roosevelt delivering the inaugural address for his second term in office*

# A Second Term

When Theodore Roosevelt was elected for his second term as president in 1904, the Roosevelts were probably the best-known family in the world—more popular even than England's royal family. People the world over seemed fascinated by the adventures of America's president. He was possibly the best-loved American president after Washington and Lincoln. And photographs of his brood of children—the famous "White House gang"—were published in papers and magazines the world over.

Roosevelt was 46 in November 1904 when he was elected president. The inauguration took place on March 4, 1905.

Roosevelt continued to uphold traditional values. At the same time he broke new ground. Roosevelt was the first president to appoint a Jew to his cabinet. In 1906 Oscar Straus became his secretary of commerce and labor. Also, soon after becoming president, Roosevelt and his wife entertained the black leader Booker T. Washington at the White House. Many people—particularly Southerners—were shocked by this modern, liberal action.

Also in 1906 Roosevelt made popular the use of the term "muckraker," for journalists and other writers who expose social injustices, political corruption or business abuses. The name comes from a character in John Bunyan's allegory *The Pilgrim's Progress.*

That same year Roosevelt appointed a special commission. This group confirmed the abuses rampant in America's meat-packing industry. There were unsafe and unclean conditions that included the poor treatment of workers. Upton Sinclair had brought the industry to national attention in his popular novel *The Jungle.* Roosevelt was concerned about mixing chemicals with foods and the false labeling of drugs. As a result, the Meat Inspection Act and Pure Food and Drug Act were both passed in 1906.

On December 10, 1906, Roosevelt was notified that he had won the Nobel Peace Prize. This was in recognition of his efforts to end the Russo-Japanese War. He was the first American and first of two U.S. presidents to win the prize. (Woodrow Wilson was the other.) Roosevelt gave his prize money to charity.

*Roosevelt with Russian and Japanese envoys at the 1905 Portsmouth Peace Conference. For his peace efforts he was awarded the 1906 Nobel Peace Prize.*

As he was leaving office, Roosevelt declared: "I do not believe that any president has had as thoroughly good a time as I have had, or has ever enjoyed himself as much."

# Life after the White House

On March 4, 1909, Theodore Roosevelt's term of office ended. He was then the youngest former president in American history. He was just over 50 years old. That same day he and Edith boarded a train for their Sagamore Hill estate.

But even though he was no longer president, Theodore Roosevelt remained in the public eye. He made expeditions to Africa and South America. Within three weeks of leaving the White House, Roosevelt sailed to Africa with his son Kermit. They spent ten months on an expedition sponsored by the Smithsonian Institution. There they collected specimens of African animals and plants. The entire journey took more than a year. At the end of the expedition, Edith joined her husband in a tour of Europe in April and May of 1910.

*Theodore Roosevelt on safari*

*Theodore and Edith in Egypt in 1910*

Roosevelt recounted his adventures in a series of articles for *Scribner's Magazine*. Later the articles were collected in a book called *African Game Trails*. The book proved to be one of Roosevelt's most popular and sold more than a million copies. In 1910 he published another book titled *The New Nationalism*.

Roosevelt wrote a number of books on many different topics. A complete list of his works contains some 2,000 to 3,000 individual titles. These include books, articles, pamphlets, speeches, addresses, and contributions to books of others, as well as translations. His books include works of history, biography, natural history, literature and political philosophy. Many of the more than 150,000 letters that he wrote during his lifetime are still in existence. Most are kept in collections at Harvard and the Library of Congress.

In 1912, at the Republican National Convention, Roosevelt lost the nomination to run for president once more. He did, however, run as candidate of the Progressive, or "Bull Moose," party. The party got its name when Roosevelt declared that he was still as fit as a bull moose. He may have been, but he was defeated.

In 1912 Edith breathed a hugh sigh of relief when it seemed certain that Theodore's days in politics were over. She was delighted at the prospect of not returning to the White House. She wanted to distance herself, her husband and her family from the distasteful world of politics.

On October 14, 1912, Roosevelt was on his way to a speaking engagement in Milwaukee, Wisconsin. A deranged man named John Schrank took aim and shot him in the chest. The impact of the bullet was diminished because it passed through Roosevelt's overcoat, a metal eyeglass case and his 50-page speech, which had been folded to double thickness. The bullet, however, did pierce his right side. It fractured his fourth rib and lodged near his right lung. Still Roosevelt insisted upon delivering his speech as scheduled. He spoke for more than an hour!

*The bullet that almost ended Theodore Roosevelt's life and the speech that saved it*

*Roosevelt while exploring the Amazon River*

In October 1913 Macmillan published *Theodore Roosevelt, An Autobiography*. That same month Roosevelt sailed for South America. While in South America, Roosevelt and his son Kermit joined a historic expedition. This trip followed the uncharted course of the Rio da Duvida, a major tributary of the Amazon River. The name means the River of Doubt. At the conclusion of the expedition the river was renamed the Rio Teodoro in honor of the former president.

For more than two months, the Roosevelt party explored the Brazilian jungle. The trip was both hazardous and eventful. Roosevelt contracted malaria and dysentery and suffered a major infection in his leg. His temperature rose intermittently to 105 degrees. It was feared that he would die. He lost 57 pounds on the journey. Three supply boats were lost in high waters. Food and other supplies ran low. One man drowned, and another went insane: He killed another expedition member before disappearing forever into the jungle.

But Roosevelt did not lose his taste for adventure. When the United States entered World War I in 1917, Roosevelt was 59. He wanted to gather a band of soldiers to go and fight the Germans in Europe. Many men were eager to serve with him. But President Wilson knew that Roosevelt was not in good health. Wilson refused to let him go. Still, the four Roosevelt sons proudly joined the army.

But Roosevelt's pride turned to anguish in July 1918 when he learned that his youngest son, Quentin, had been killed. Quentin, a pilot, had been shot down over Cambrai in northern France by German airmen. Roosevelt never got over his youngest son's death.

During World War I, Edith Roosevelt also made her contribution to the war effort. She served as a regional president of the Needlework Guild. As directress of the Oyster Bay chapter, she oversaw women's efforts in knitting sweaters, socks and caps for American soldiers fighting in Europe. Years later she joined other first ladies in a radio project aimed at promoting the Girl Scouts of America.

# Edith's Life Alone

Theodore Roosevelt died on January 6, 1919, of a coronary embolism. He was at home in Oyster Bay. His funeral service and burial also took place in Oyster Bay. Edith was grief-stricken, but she did not allow her husband's death to destroy her.

Following Roosevelt's death, Edith spent two decades traveling around the world. She lent her support to many worthwhile causes. One of her first projects was the recon-

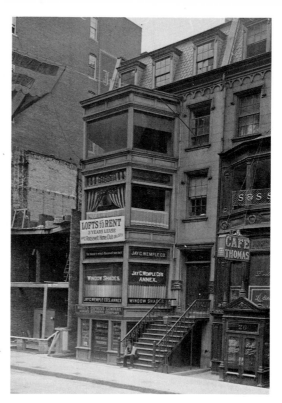

*The birthplace of Theodore Roosevelt*

struction of Theodore's birthplace. On East 20th Street in New York City, visitors can see a house very much like the one where young Theodore grew up. Roosevelt's original childhood home had been torn down, but the home now is a close replica of the birthplace. The rebuilding of the house was supervised by Roosevelt's widow and his two surviving sisters. It was opened to the public in 1923.

Some of the furniture in the house is from the original birthplace. Included is the bed in which Roosevelt and his brother and sisters were born. Next to one of the fireplaces is the small velvet chair where he read as a child. Most of the other furniture is from other Roosevelt family homes of the time. Attached to the house are two rooms that display many souvenirs of the Roosevelt family.

43

Strangely, Edith made her first public speech during the 1932 presidential election campaigns. Mortified that many people assumed that Franklin D. Roosevelt was her son or grandson, the forceful former first lady addressed a huge crowd assembled at Madison Square Garden. She urged voters to cast their ballots not for her nephew-in-law Franklin Roosevelt, but for his Republican opponent, Herbert Hoover.

On her 80th birthday in 1941, the *New York Times* had written of Edith: "This is a great as well as a beloved woman." But soon her health began to fail. On September 30, 1948, Edith Roosevelt died. She was 87. Edith was buried next to her husband in Young's Cemetery in Oyster Bay, not far from the Sagamore Hill estate.

*Edith Roosevelt in 1934*

# For Further Reading

Fisher, Leonard Everett. *The White House.* New York: Holiday House, 1989.

Force, Eden. *Theodore Roosevelt.* New York: Franklin Watts, 1987.

Friedel, Frank. *The Presidents of the United States of America.* Revised edition. Washington, D.C.: The White House Historical Association, 1989.

Hagedorn, Hermann. *The Roosevelts of Sagamore Hill.* New York: The Macmillan Company, 1954.

*The Living White House.* Revised edition. Washington, D.C.: The White House Historical Association, 1987.

McCullough, David. *Mornings on Horseback.* New York: Simon & Schuster, 1981.

Menendez, Albert J. *Christmas in the White House.* Philadelphia: The Westminster Press, 1983.

Morris, Edmund. *The Rise of Theodore Roosevelt.* New York: Coward McCann Geoghan, 1979.

Morris, Sylvia Jukes. *Edith Kermit Roosevelt.* New York: Coward McCann Geoghan, 1980.

St. George, Judith. *The White House: Cornerstone of a Nation.* New York: G. P. Putnam's Sons, 1990.

# Index